North East Passage

Scottish Contemporary Poets Series

(for further details of this series please contact the publishers)

Gerry Cambridge, *The Shell House;* 1 898218 34 X
Jenni Daiches, *Mediterranean;* 1 898218 35 8
Valerie Gillies, *The Ringing Rock;* 1 898218 36 6
Kenneth Steven, *The Missing Days;* 1 898218 37 4
Brian Johnstone, *The Lizard Silence;* 1 898218 54 4
Siùsaidh NicNèill, *All My Braided Colours;* 1 898218 55 2
Ken Morrice, *Talking of Michelangelo;* 1 898218 56 0
Tom Bryan, *North East Passage;* 1 898218 57 9
Maureen Sangster, *Out of the Urn;* 1 898218 65 X
Anne MacLeod, *Standing by Thistles;* 1 898218 66 8
Walter Perrie, *From Milady's Wood;* 1 898218 67 6
William Hershaw, *The Cowdenbeath Man;* 1 898218 68 4

North East Passage

Tom Bryan

SCOTTISH CONTEMPORARY POETS SERIES

SCOTTISH CULTURAL PRESS

First published 1996
by Scottish Cultural Press
PO Box 106, Aberdeen AB11 7ZE
Tel: 01224 583777
Fax: 01224 575337

British Library Cataloguing in Publication Data
A catalogue for this book is available from the British Library

ISBN: 1 898218 57 9

The publisher acknowledges subsidy from the Scottish Arts Council
towards the publication of this book

Printed and bound by
BPC-AUP Aberdeen Ltd.

Contents

Tom Bryan was born in Manitoba, Canada, in 1950 but has been long-resident in Scotland. His poems and stories have been widely published in several countries and he has written many articles for newspapers and magazines. His collection *Wolfwind* was published by Chapman, Edinburgh.

He has worked at a wide variety of jobs over the years, ranging from steeplejack to salmon farmer. Most recently, he has been Writer-in-Residence for Banff and Buchan District Council. He also edits the literary magazine *Northwords,* which has given much encouragement to prose and poetry in Scots, Gaelic and English.

He is married with two children and lives in Strathkanaird, Wester Ross.

Acknowledgements

This collection of poems was written during my tenure as Writer-in-Residence for Banff and Buchan District Council, 1994–1996. Although based in Macduff, my job took me to all corners of the district, in all seasons and weathers, to work with writers from Peterhead to Portsoy, the Broch to Fyvie. I learned a great deal too, about the history, culture and language of the North East: a culture I had already aquired a great respect for. These are not the poems of an expert on life in the North East; hardly – but they are the record, a diary almost, of an eager traveller and sojourner. I would like to thank all the people who received me with great North East hospitality and to those in the District Council who made my work possible, particularly Iain MacAulay, Arts Development Officer for the district. Many of the poems have the theme of exile; a familiar theme to Scots at home and abroad. I've tried to include poems on North East characters who have made contributions all over the globe. I would also like to thank the Scottish Arts Council for their support of these residencies which permit teaching and learning to take place. Special thanks also to Alan Patterson and Max Pittman for computing advice and help.

At the time of this acknowledgement, all poems in this collection were previously unpublished.

Poems not dealing directly with North East life were written during my time of residence there.

This book is dedicated to all the folk of the North East with whom I worked.

I High Streets and Low

Banff

The sea stole away to Macduff
leaving sea-wealth stranded.
Redundant clipper-ship captains
dreamt seaward
watching, windward, waiting.

Janus-face,
sea lapping at ships and shipyards
across the river;
a separate psyche,
schizophrenic:
white/black
Athens/Sparta
banker/shipwright.

Legend says
folk here couldn't wait
to hang the gypsy fiddler –
tampered with time to cheat reprieve.

As the River Deveron
dumped sand like an hourglass,
the sea silted away to Macduff.

Macduff

(note: Macpherson, the gypsy fiddler, was hung in Banff, to the disgust of Macduff people. Legend states that folk in Banff turned their official clock forward to hasten the fiddler's execution, and to cheat the expected reprieve on its way across the Deveron from Macduff, where Macpherson was generally welcome.)

'Dead Slow' says the breakwater sign.
Doric in dawn's drizzle, sea smashes,
sea wall holds.
Esau town,
hard-working twin.
Banff is the favoured older sister.
We see it everywhere:
Glasgow/Edinburgh
Rotterdam/Amsterdam.
Do not be fooled:
what you see is not all there is.

Macpherson wasn't hung here –
between gospel and bingo hall,
shipyard and pub,
Macduff folk had time for fiddling gypsies,
still do.

Fishermen who float on millennia
don't fiddle with minutes.

Montcoffer Sequence

Bed in room, room in house.
House in forest.
Chestnut tree, taller than the house.
Yew tree, older.
Monkey puzzle, more exotic.
Beech, bolder, as thrawn.

1) Buzzard of morning
blocks my window,
fluffing pride, young on the bough.
In winter,
worries the branch
where chestnuts will come.
I can barely see sky for tree.
Bird can't see me.
Pity – for
the palsied rabbit
did not see you.

2) Big house dwarfed by birdsong.
A song bigger than a house?
Easy.
Peesie.
Listen to the lapwing.

3) Leaf/barley/river/field.
Salmon struggle
up moonsplash arteries.
I tell you – salmon do spawn in barley fields.
These are strange days,
from my window.

4) Life lingers
in winter wind.
I stare hard
at a tree's green centuries.

5) I saw a pulsing riot
of leaves.
Ice wrapped grass blades
in hard sheathes.
Gorse gloated
like a fat man counting gold.
Snowdrops huddled in igloos.

6) Green burbled chlorophyll volcanoes.
Flowers puked purples,
yellows and reds.
Summer came and came.

Fraserburgh

Foundations built on fish
and deep-sea dreams.
Wounds cauterised by sharp salt.
Packed kists
bound for Stornoway, Lerwick, Lowestoft,
Fingers blue with cold
tied their own dreams in bundles.
Look at the old photographs,
dark eyes outsparkle
any silver fish.

Yet they packed their kist
for a future that never came.
Silver darlings sank deep
in the blood of Empire.
Fish-bloodied hands
would have other killing work to do.

Look at the old photographs;
look at the eyes
they knew what was coming
they knew.

Deer Abbey

Cumulus roof,
nimbus windows,
cirrus walls.
Butterflies pray,
milk cows queue
at the crow confessional.
Liturgical weeds
spill into holy ground.

I walk the grass in city shoes
whose idling soles
blaspheme the silence.

Men drank here,
kept bees,
surely dreamt
of tribal milkmaids.

They made a Celtic book
when these walls were young,
shining summers ago.
Abbey crumbled on the hill –
the book is with us still.

Peterhead

Blue Toon – blues tuned
by flick-knife rain.
Granite, red-bricked,
oil-licked.
Petroleum baked haddock,
barnacled to deep water.

It is all – out there,
brought back to bedsit.
Hail falling doon like blues,
in the Blue Toon.

Bruising bottleneck
of profit and loss
on a shifting slag sea;

Woke up this morning
and every morning, waking up
to blues spewed like sea-sickness
on dark, slow-rolling blue.

Peterhead Prison
(for the Invernettie Writers Group)

While free men fish
and seal pup sings,
the prison clings to the harbour
like a tired barnacle.

Limpet, ready to let go
and surrender to the rain.
Stone walls – no barrier
to poetry or redemption.

Prisoners write about injured seagulls,
love and birthdays
life before here.

Meanwhile, the limpet is letting go.
Reborn as a bird of the air,
a freestyle fish, a faraway foghorn
on a ship, Africa-bound.

They are on board
a magic carpet,

woven from barbwire.

Turriff

Sweet treacly coffee and a crumbling scone,
mist lifting from November noon,
Turriff, Indian summer's
ripe plump apple –
fulsome harvest in a bulging land.
Hearing words planted
by Viking seedsmen,
centuries of nurture,
lifetimes in the furrow,
cold steel words
from luscious soil,
grafted to ancient rock,
ripening still.

II   October Roads

October Road, Buchan

These stitched stubble fields
belong to no place or time.
I've seen them in Monet,
in Iraq,
in the spluttered leaf-bleeding
American Fall.
Pheasants stick postage stamp colour
to odd corners of this earthen envelope.

The crows belong anywhere too:
velvet criminals, spies, purple pickpockets,
cackling contempt into salt-wind.

And around a bend
on a house gable of wind-clarted stone,
three wooden butterflies are nailed:
Blue
Green
Yellow

Brittle, fragile, absurd
in this Buchan chill where grey rules, OK?

Yet they belong
windward to the blasting rain.

Thrawn – crucified
they bide.

Buchan in Buckskin

(for Duncan McLean)

North East shit-kickers
in glowering gorse
which looks like Texas tumbleweed to me.
Ain't no cotton along the Deveron –
Chevvies rust on the Ythan.

Red-neck, Gamrie style.
Tattooed knuckles: 'LOVE' 'HATE'
'ABERDEEN FOOTBALL CLUB'.

White trash, poor boy,
hard work and harder fun.
Codfish to Cotton,
Haddock to Lubbock.

White Man's Blues in Doric Drawl.
Western Swing come home?

No, it never left.

Buchan Roadhouse Blues

Buddy Guy blues, late night BBC.
Driving, Broch to Banff.
Chicago – blizzards away.
The Windy City shivers,
stirks are shivering too.
This winter night is blue.

The salt wind fillets –
my memories.
In the North East,
no need for metaphor:
Hail falls doon – like Hail, ken?
Blues is blue is blue.

Buddy, rip your blues.
Sizzle our skulls.
Chicago or Buchan,
this frozen field
is the 'Ice Man's' yield.

And all over the world,
we drive the dark blue night.

The Chalmers Hospital, Banff

Eightfold path, not Buddha,
but window panes.
Four on the right –
sky, from sludge to blue.
Three top left,
soiled stone and slate.
Bottom left,
one injured young seagull.

I may be a poet
but bird is a painter:
sky-slung shit
on the red Porsche below,
white streaks
on a posh palette.

Scavenger fixes
a baleful eye on me;
keeks seaward,
flexes her wings.
Her flight
would fill my window
with cold rain.

I too must fly again.

Coastal Spring

Crocus-splattered grass verge,
splurge of dribbled rainbow.
Sea waves churning, creaming,
breezes lifting flowered frocks.

Ground is growling
in warming furrows
and
one lark is perched
on a stop light, turning red.
Her trilling stops
the traffic dead.

Desert Rain
(for Miguel Padilla)

Far from
banana blossom fragrance
and lush avocado hills,
further from
the poetry of place –
savour these, chew them slowly:

Cimarron
Conchas
Arroyo Hondo
Tularosa
Jicarilla
Sangre de Cristo.

A painter/musician/alchemist
conjures sauces and spices
in a kitchen of remembrance.
Hear the rattlesnakes
shaking on Turra pavements.
See the pale adobe
shivering in Scottish rain.

Buchan skies are cold and grey
while avocados ripen, planets away.

But home is a hunger
that can be fed,
an aroma that can be painted.

False Spring, Buchan

Yellow gorse
fooled by yellow sun.
Green bud fist,
impatient for April,
in January.

Broom bush, wiser plant,
feels false warmth.
Ephemeral heat of
winter's suck and blow.
Plant knuckles
chappin patiently
on doors of ice.

Famous

A shotgun sprinkle of freckles
fidgeting got straight to the point:
Mr Bryan, Tom, Sir
'Are you…are you FAMOUS?'
Her face floated,
freckles scrunched in suspense.
She wanted me to be – famous.

I thought of our boyhood joke;
'World famous – in Canada.'
Our heroes were local and obscure.
I'll test you.
Gordie Howe?
Boom-Boom Geoffrion?
Rocket Richard?
Hank Snow?
No?
I told you so.

And what did Dylan Thomas declare:
He was 'famous among the barns.'
I too remember four decades of barns and byres
who don't remember me…moreover,
I wasn't even famous
among bales of sweetgrass and clover.

Meanwhile, a frown is digging a freckled furrow.
Keats on fame: 'what is fame but a slow decay?'
And this pert questioner will be in her prime
when I am well decayed; not famous – just 'not.'
She needs an answer quick, the right one.

'Yes,' I smile with benign look
'I am famous in a Strath
where the trout and birches ken me well.
I'd be glad to sign your book.'

And her freckles grin and frolic.
I autograph her school jotter,
my name alongside an injured striker
from Deveronvale Football Club – who
is world famous – in Banff.
We both belong on that crowded page.
Writers – like wingers – get bruised black and blue,
and poets – like footballers – get relegated too.
While her freckles exploded in suns of laughter,
for five full seconds, I truly felt fame.

He Said

The lime-green beech
darkens overnight
to a hard blue sheen.

The wind then snaps branches
in another key. Frets the leaves
to another tuning.

Seasons shift by the minute,
the wind turns.
Listen for a final flattened seventh,
the blues chord –
you won't hear it coming.

Magpies in Snow Blizzard

Remind me the rhyme of magpie luck.
Good luck or bad.
Eight magpies in a hawthorn hedge.
Black feathers, white blizzard –
huddling for heat.

'Eight' for survival
'Black' for breath
'White' for snow
'Ice' for death.

May Moon, Macduff

Tangerine teeters on a pine tree top.
Psychedelic citrus
on a madman's romp.
Far out fruit on a be-bop hop.

Cheddar balloon in lunatic land,
loups hedgerow bunnies,
badger and deer.
Full moon fantasy for a one-moon band.

Moonlight lovers just gawk tonight
at this floating nocturnal nectarine.
While shite-soaked scarecrows blow
wild sax in orange juice light.

A moon fingers could slice or peel,
a moon with a smiling simpleton face.
Low enough for a cow to be leaping,
And if a werewolf howls, his song is ***real.***

Neil Paterson (1915–1995)

'I miss Banff. It will always be home to me. I have a very soft spot for
Macduff.'

(letter from Neil Paterson, 10 March, 1995)

Small Scottish boys
climb slippery seawalls,
and graze their dreams
on granite.

Boy becomes man.
He trawls the world:
Spain
Saskatchewan
Hollywood.

Far East of fiction,
swinging on trapezes,
mastering the matador's art,
restless, rooted, returning.

Small boys in Scotland
still spit into the salt wind:
and grow
to captain football teams,
fight wars, father children,
win Oscars.

As long as our dreams outlast our dust,
dreamers will peer at the world
over cold stone walls,
ride Clipper ships to Shanghai,
but come home,
at last,
to sleep.

North, by North-East
(for S.G.)

The North West Passage
is a personal rite of passage,
on no map drawn;
A snowshoe trek
begun in a boy's mind.
A traveller's tongue
wraps around new words,
new worlds.
A Yukon blizzard might bring memories
of a three pence poke of chips,
or the sight of winter barley.
Lynx, wolverine, cougar and bear
provoke the peesies.
Chinook in one ear,
curlew in the other.

Fine fur trapper,
now fine trapper of words.

North East Big Cat

From the Broch to Ballater,
hard ground, hard fact.
'Fancy' is confined to bakeries,
what you see – will always be.

But tell that to the muckle cat.
One day, yowe-ripping at Old Deer,
next day prowling
Huntly's howling shed.

Yellow-eyed panther
in winter's yellow gorse,
shrieking at the hard edge
of the Blue Toon.

Yet loons having no time
to waste on dreaming
plough deep Buchan earth
near the jungle rim,
yearning for just a glimpse
of that frenzied 'fiction'.

North East Hill Farm

Wind-bevelled trees dovetail
to a sludge cloud frontier.
Dust-familiar outbuildings
fade to stony outcrop,
mortgaged only to wind and rain.

Winter barley ebbs and eddies
in deep beige pools.

Peesies stumble sunward
in their clumsy, perfect roll and pitch.
Rusting tractors shelter magpies in a weed-choked ditch.

Aberdeen Family History Centre

Crowded microfilm cloister
in the hurly-burly of bookmakers,
chippie, newsagent,

Emigrations, mistakes, disruptions –
leap from stale files;
families dance fiddling
from Cairnbulg to California,
Boddam to Broken Fork.
Lives strewn and blown
across desert and sea,
like the litter
I see through these fading
Venetian blinds.

Pittodrie Winter, 4.45 pm

Grass under shellac of ice,
ball skites wide,
always out of touch.
Sky oily black
while European memories
float from floodlit haze.

Brown puddles form where a man could drown,
one last chance is knocked to touch,
cold rain keeps falling down.

Sunset Song, Revisited

I swear I saw Meikleboggs, yesterday,
fumbling with his trouser fly,
spitting at the sun.

Mutch was there too,
nose a 'dreep,
polishing his shopfront brass.

Long Rob strides high in the parks,
while John Guthrie wrestles with
seed-time devils.

I collided with Colquhoun's
rusted bike on his vision road.

Wind-bent trees sway
to growling cello chords.

And I saw proud Chris Guthrie
at Tesco's today,
pushing a frozen food trolley,
her body strong and ripe.

It is still a rich human silage (and slurry too)
Rain clouds yet darken the howe.
And Gibbon, listen
peesies still sing
to the sea.

Unknown Rivers

Deveron ripples jigs and reels,
zig-zags
to a final brutal swelling.

I conjure
mile-wide mud,
King Kong rivers,
breaking levees,
like mud castles.

Bluesmen cross my dream rivers,
and play bottleneck
on sun-blistered porches.

Molasses rivers host
no rich man's salmon beat.

When I dream rivers,
I dream cool deep mud.

Dead Sperm Whales, Cruden Bay

People rounded the cordon,
just to stroke these
great slabs of power,
turning putrid.

While scientists sought
reason's black box,
six tribal compasses exploded
in broken galaxies;
ambergris astrolabes
bled totemic maps.

This cold Cruden rock:

not the sweet hay of Sargasso
not the crunch of deep-dwelling Kraken
not the flesh of great fish
off Patagonia.

Terra incognita to flickering brains
fallen off the edge of known Oceans.

Scrimshaw eulogy,
bulldozed mausoleum.

A pit *could* be dug, at a cost of X.

III Sonnets of Steerage

James Gordon Bennett

Born Newmill, Keith, 1795. Died New York City, 1872. Colourful New York City journalist and editor. Fierce defender of freedom of the press.

Jamie, frae Keith, awa tae Aiberdeen tae be a priest,
sidetracked, starving in New York – the fool!
Hack journalist, notorious, known not least
to the New York Enquirer. Replaced its editor (shot in a duel)
In 1835, Bennett founded the New York Herald,
with a plank, two flour barrels: a desk to prop his feet.
'One poor man in a cellar – against the world'
he declared. He was punched, spat on in the street.

New York marvelled at this Banffshire vandal
Who kept his own dispatch boats and telegraph crews.
Who filled his paper 'with vulgarity, vituperation and
            scandal...'
but his critics admitted: 'he got the news.'

'Obscene foreign vagabond' enemies hissed through their
            teeth.
Yet – national hero, defender of freedom – this mannie frae
            Keith.

Alexander Cuming

Born, Culter, Aberdeenshire, 1690. Died a pauper in London's Charterhouse Hospital, 1775. Adventurer, alchemist, crowned 'Emperor of the Cherokees', planned a Jewish nation in America.

Second Baronet of Culter, Captain in the Russian Army.
Walter Mitty eccentric, dreamer, schemer, ranter, raver.
Went to collect plants in Carolina, considered barmy.
Convinced the Cherokee he was their Emperor and Saviour.
Cherokee on bended knee – humour him – they reckoned,
crowned him 'Emperor of the Cherokee' – their Wilderness
        King.
He took seven Indian braves to visit George the Second,
Wined, dined, feted; but the Crown grew bored with this
        'Emperor' thing.

Cuming's career sunk down and down,
Had a vision of a Jewish homeland which couldn't fail,
Cuming was convicted of fraud, called a clown,
Was arrested and thrown in jail.

Nearly thirty years in Fleet Prison, transferred to a Poorhouse
        bed.
Mind gone, babbling of the Cherokee mountains – they found
        him dead.

Thomas Davidson

Born Old Deer Parish, 1840. Died New York, 1900. Scholar, philosopher, writer, teacher, social reformer.

Fairmer's loon who read every book in Old Deer,
Saint's Rest by Baxter, his beacon and shining light.
Scholarships, bursaries, classical scholar without peer.
London, Canada, America – the philosopher took flight.
Became a Missouri Marxist, this restless young gypsy,
then lived in the Italian mountains as a religious hermit.
Back to London, became a Socialist in eighteen eighty-three.
Bought a hill farm in the Adirondacks and a fire was lit.

Adult slum teacher in New York's Lower East Side,
Taught refugees and immigrants philosophy and art.
This Old Deer lad embraced the emigant tide,
Speaking their tongue – his mind never ruled his heart.

To New York concrete from Old Deer's Holy Ground,
Tom Davidson – scholar gypsy – sought; in seeking, found.

Alexander Garden

Born Birse Parish, circa 1730. Died 1791. Naturalist and physician in South Carolina; classified many new fauna and flora in America.

Boy of the Manse, he sang Birse Parish names.
Gaelic/Doric mixter-maxter, Brackenstake to Auchnafoy.
On forest and river he made his claims,
Sailed to South Carolina in medical employ.
A hero against smallpox, grew famous and rich,
describing animals never named before:
He wrote of an electric eel in a muddy ditch,
while Europeans scoffed at such backwoods 'lore.'

Garden was loyal to the Crown, stuck to his botany.
Banished, threatened, life out on a limb.
Escaped to England, coughing blood, terminal TB.
A true memorial: the Gardenia was named for him.

Quote: 'Georgian gentleman, refined.' (the height of sobriety)
'Fond of good company…and refined female society.'

George Grant

*Born rural Banffshire, circa 1810. Died on the Kansas prairie, 1878.
Grant was a wealthy merchant who founded a colony termed 'Little
England' in the wilds of Kansas.*

Lad o'pairts, smooth talkin' Banffshire 'wideboy',
Cornered the black crepe market when Prince Albert died,
wealthy silk merchant wanted to retire and enjoy,
He looked around. In fertile Kansas he'd bide.
He founded Victoria, craftily named for Her Majesty,
watering hole for wealthy wastrels to do as they please.
It was all there: manor homes, hunting lodges for the gentry,
wine cellars, imported English wildlife, exotic fruit trees.

Colony for cast-offs of the landed classes,
'playboys, remittance men with allowances,' money to burn.
Red coats, high boots, with leisure to sit on their arses,
Grant died. Soon the colony wasn't worth a durn.

Kansas of sunflowers on prairies the colour of rust.
George Grant's dream foundered, was shrouded over with
        dust.

William Keith

Born, Old Meldrum, 1839. Died, California, 1911. Keith was a famous landscape painter and conservationist in the Yosemite wilderness. He was a close friend of the great environmentalist John Muir from Dunbar and deserves to be as famous.

Small boy's footprints on the emigrant trail,
Old Meldrum, Whiterashes, to Aberdeen.
Across the ocean and beyond the pale,
Young Keith could sketch, could draw a scene.
Worked for the Northern Pacific, sketchbook in hand.
Keith studied in Europe but studied life in the wild.
Tramped with John Muir over Indian land.
Looked at the wilderness like a newborn child.

Colour, flower, rocky gorge, shadow and sunshine.
Artist/prophet of the giant Redwood.
Memorising mountains, every feature and line,
in his dying years, painted every tree he could.

In Old Meldrum his eye was sharpened by cloud and rain.
In old age, by Sonora's moon-mountain terrain.

Hugh Mercer

Born, Aberdeen, 1725. A Jacobite surgeon who survived Culloden, fled to America, and died fighting for George Washington's Revolutionary Army, in New Jersey, 1777.

Mercer learned surgery in Aberdeen,
Studied butchery at Culloden,
Fled, price on his head, only nineteen,
Fought in the Indian wars with frontier men.
Respected Virginia doctor and apothecary,
Trained the 'Minute Men' and was given command,
Abandoned the scalpel, became a revolutionary,
Led the 'Flying Camp' – ragtag fighting band.

Mercer's were tactics of guerrilla war,
at Stony Brook, Princeton and Delaware.
Horse killed, Mercer was clubbed to the ground and bore
seven bayonet wounds, yet didn't die there.

Mercer took nine full days to bleed to death,
Cursed the House of Hanover with his dying breath.

James 'Scotty' Philip

Born, 1858, Auchness Farm, Dallas, Morayshire. Died circa 1910. Philip had many true adventures in the Wild West. He was credited with saving the American buffalo from certain extinction. He was very sympathetic to the plight of Native Americans and was the great Sioux warrior Crazy Horse's brother-in-law.

Farm boy went West at the age of sixteen,
into the Black Hills to pan for gold.
Gave it his all but was 'busted clean.'
Left Dakota when he was nineteen years old.
Forget Hollywood and its Wild West lie,
Scotty Philip swashbuckled a true life of his own,
he sadly watched Cheyenne warriors die,
his relative, Crazy Horse, was murdered alone.

Scotty said 'they were broken in spirit and health.'
Jamie Philip saw the meaning of genocide,
how the buffalo was the source of the Red Man's wealth,
Scotty bought buffalo and helped them bide.

Scotty Philip: 'The Buffalo King,' a Moray man.
He saved the buffalo – who couldn't save the Cheyenne.

George Stephen

Born 1829, in Banffshire, grew up in Dufftown. Became a banker and was founder of the Canadian Pacific Railway, which joined Canada together and had a profound impact on that nation's future.

The Canadian Pacific began in Dufftown,
Its founder, George Stephen, was nurtured there.
Aberdeen to London, he'd been around.
With his cousin, became Canada's railroad pair.
Railway. THWACK. Slavs hammering cold steel.
Railway. THWACK. Scandinavians break hard rock.
German straw bosses with wounds to heal.
Irish poker players, Chinese with opium to hock.

Bare-knuckle boxing, horseshoes, tug-of-war.
THWACK. Backs breaking, laying steel on grass.
Stephen faced bankruptcy; they'd loan no more.
But workers drove the final spike in Eagle Pass.

From Dufftown to the Pacific on a dragon of steam.
The Canadian Pacific: a Dufftown dream.

IV Other Maps

Galloway Heat Wave

Slow-motion mink seek cold slate shelter,
Rabbits reel on hot tar roads,
Blackbirds batten down in bracken,
Hawks baste above barley swelter.

Dry thistles thirst for raindrop tea
Parched land teased by a slime-green sea.

Jekyll/Hyde
(The Meadows, Edinburgh, 1995)

Meths men puke near the Whalebone Arch,
student skirts whipped thigh high by the wind –
visual feast for the dipso dull –
slurping cheap wine from the good doctor's skull.

Wrapping his lechery in a brown paper bag,
Hyde gropes the gutters for a hard-earned fag.

Lockerbie, Summer, 1995

Honeybees suck flowerbeds,
Hills haloed by fruit and grain,
New grass gauze for hillside scars,
A child skips in cleansing rain.

Western Passage
(A Harris/Lewis sequence, Summer, 1995)

1) Derelict Whaling Station, Bunaveneadar

Brick smokestack, tangible,
poised above shimmering loch: the whale road.
Ending here, for flensing and boiling down.
A century ago, they towed a great blue beast
for boiling, oil for a thousand island nights.
Oil for memory, flickering and fickle,
fires smoored finally by thistle and bracken.
That makes three gravestones:
memory
smokestack
The third, in Norwegian, for a much-loved dog.

2) Luskentyre

'Beach' is not dignified enough,
nor 'desert', for this Sahara of polished stone
and azure shell,
trailing to all horizons.

Razor shells gleam like ivory piano keys,
while sea trout snap
at a savoury moon.

3) Leverburgh Sabbath

Churches: a horseshoe of three.
Full except for some clouds and me.
Fat trout flop in the kirkside sea.
The wind wails psalms through a willow tree.

4) Lewis Lighthouse

Lovers' lane
where a discarded bra
formed two perfect hills
between lighthouse and sea.

A Minch away,
Suilven was likewise a miniature
lavender D-cup
on a twilight shore.

Like wet stones in a burn,
dolphin backs invite me to cross.

Moonlit distortion complete:
lighthouse, white bra peaks
and a living bridge to Sutherland.

5) Finding a Poet's Address (for Ian Stephen)

Turn left at a larch hull,
find the function
of a former telephone box
turned greenhouse.

Roof of living turf,
more windows than doors.

Here a poet lives and works.

6) Leaving the Long Island

It's only fair –
this gossamer clothesline of thought.
From The Clisham to Suilven –
I've seen Harris from over there.

A world now drawn to perfect scale
(In the teacup of a languid Minch)
Cul Beag lunges above my house,
Stornoway to Canisp on the back of a whale.

A Forest Hut

(based on anonymous tenth century poem in Irish)

Evil man, tax man, my hut is not on your map or list.
It is small yet opens to the universe – will you see it friend?
My sanctuary.

Ceiling? Blue or grey – as the shifting clouds.

Walls? Of living larch, hollow elder, bursting butterfly bush.
Living wood, not planed or smoothed. My walls blossom,
shed leaves, bend in the winter, droop with snow.

Floor? Carpet of herbs, azure and sweet grass. Crossroads
carpet, soft on the nimble feet of red deer, comical hedgehog,
alert fox, volatile badger; hiding place for leather adder and
darting lizard. My floor is cleaned by the red muscled stags of
Meall a'Chuaille, Ruith Chnoc, Creag na h'Iolaire; by the shy
hinds of the tall grasses.

My food is free, within these walls: rough-skinned apples,
bittersweet plums, dark cherries, ripe blaeberries, flopping fat
rhubarb.

The water here is a sweet wine; it comes from pebbles of
shining gold in the sun, deep silver in the cold rain.

My walls and ceilings sing. Listen. Living wood grows,
growth itself is a song. Larch hums, ash crackles, the hollow
elder makes fine flutes; rowan sighs, willow whispers, birch
dances in the wind to all music-making.

My hut is refuge to the bounding lamb, the wary cat, the
sniffing sheepdog, the runaway dun calf. All these are
welcome, to stay or go.

Summer herbs freshen the air of the hut: water-loving mint,
lemon balm, southern wood, bitter chives, tangy nettles.
Elderflower mead – lemon-like, thirst-slaking, quenching
bubbles for a hermit's tongue.

Birds play in my moving walls: throaty thrush, gargling in the morning. Blackbird of the trembling note; raucous gulls, cackling starlings, velvet swallows, woodcocks; all warble within, and welcome.

Smaller visitors from smaller universes; scurrying beetles; the paintings on my wall are sleeping butterflies; red admirals on their long journeys. Soft wings of white, deep orange, bright yellow; these tiny paintings breathe briefly on my walls.

My hut is an orchestra: wind chimes, bird melody, the gentle-flowing river; cymbals of crashing thunder, hushed vespers of evening birdsong.

My hut is both priceless and worthless. There is gold in the ceiling: Sun and Moon. Silver in the walls: cold rain. Emerald floor of shimmering grass. All priceless and worthless.

Hut far from noise, quarrel and strife. My hut is much wider than a coffin, many times wider than a church door. Enter my hut, friend. Do you see walls where others see none? Orion is my roof. Do you hear the music within these walls? If so, welcome to my hut, stranger, for it is really the wide universe.

The Wall Above my Writing Desk
(with apologies to the sonnet form)

I

To some it is a mess beyond the duster,
a vomited collage of colour and chaos,
effervescent like a bubbling gas,
to me a symbol of life's noise and bluster.
It is a cosmos – a universe in cluster,
as incoherent as midnight radio jazz
with every trait that anarchy has –
in every corner space can muster.
Start at the rafter and let the eye work down:
posters of blues singers long since dead,
Red Clydeside next to a vaudeville clown.
Men and women, yellow, white and red
who have paid dues to the hellhound,
and have kicked back, and bled.

II

Mine is also a musical wall:
an Irishman has scrawled a jig and reel:
next to a Hendrix ticket that has begun to peel;
Blues, folk and Country – room here for all.
Poems copied longhand stretching ten feet tall,
tacked next to a drawing of a lobster creel.
(Aye, see him, his colour sense isnae real!)
Things floating, gravity says should fall.
Photos and postcards of harp and guitar,
badges and souvenirs from festivals and gigs,
Buttons from Dublin, pub and bar.
Sketches of birds, fish, clocks and pigs.
Paintings and charcoal from near and far.
Next to a man on the North Sea rigs.

III

All the world comes here to climb my wall,
a poem from Wales to banish hares from my peas,
a water colour from the Antipodes,
a Pictish maze from a Rhineland stall.
A yellow leaf from an Indiana Fall.
A banjo-mandolin from a soldier Scot,
A ceramic flute from that Lancashire lot,
A badge, in Russian, from Lake Baikal.
A beer mat arrived here from Yellowknife
along with a bronze from County Clare;
an old ferry ticket (Fishguard to Rosslare)
Some snapshots which actually belong to my wife.
(One of an old red kiosk, no longer there.)

IV

Photos? Five generations of my blood and bone,
Ireland to Canada, farmers of wheat,
in sepia photo, Saskatchewan snow and sleet.
Six brothers, all dead, my father was one.
I too am captured, perched on Sutherland stone,
cooking brown trout over a fire of peat
(throwing ones back too small to eat)
But cleaners, sanitisers, let my wall alone!
I banish you like the sons of Cain!
Tidy men, my wall is the breath of me.
What agitates you, keeps me sane.
Give over, you advocates of symmetry!
Don't preach a monochrome refrain,
For if walls can be doors, then let in the rain!

Children of the Raven

There are over 53,000 persons of the surname 'Bryan' in North America, but are outnumbered world-wide by the 'O'Briens' by a five to one margin. Where did my probable 'O' go?

Was it dropped in a waterlogged bundle at Ballysteen or
     Kilgrogan,
quietly forgotten in a mad rush for the emigrant ship?
Was it blown away on the dusty famine road to an tOilean Ur
    – the New World?
Or simply ditched at Ara, Shanagolden or Ballynaskreena?

Starving men have bartered more than names.
Surnames are hurdles, hard baggage.
Was it tossed overboard from the fever ships,
the way child coffins were?
Did it slip down easily, shark fodder on the whale-road?

I imagine a soft green 'O' floating like Sargasso weed,
a homing instinct driving it back to a secluded Donegal
     headland,
where it blossoms yet as a sacred oak.
Or, floating like Brendan's dream, witness to sea serpents,
fiery stars, holy visions and maritime miracles.
Westering, gliding as a silent canoe over the water maps
of Cabot and Cartier, slipping into Canadian creeks
and dark Micmac forests.

Maybe the good citizens of Montreal wouldn't permit it
     ashore,
leaving it to float in fever hospitals
until typhus took it down.
Name-shorn survivors had the 'O' surgically removed
by Anglophile and monoglot immigration officers
who thought it politically scruffy and suspect,
turning these Irish men and women out like urchins with new
     haircuts,
blinking in the Canadian sun, now safe for Saxon Empire:
Byrne, Bryan, Brennan, Hanlon.

But maybe the O was never there in the first place.
Bryan logically precedes O'Brien: out of Bryan, of Bryan.
Hear the ancient evidence:
'Sea horses glisten in summer,
as far as Bran stretched his glance,
rivers pour forth a stream of honey,
in the Land of Mananna, son of Ler.'
Irish Bran, the fierce hound of Finn, 'poor and black, raven.'
Raven God of the Celtic underworld, namesake of carnage,
joyous jackal but skilled also in the harp
'and seven times seven musical instruments.'

Brian, crafty son of Tuirenn, Brian the slayer of the Sun God.
Bryan-Welsh Bryn-mountain dweller, mountain man.
Sun-killer, mountain dweller, child of the raven.
Myself – out of Ireland, ova, outward, out and off,
over the waves in another century,
to Ontario: beginning and ending with O – alpha and omega,

ancient prefix,

full circle.

Borderline

Eliding, slurring,
speech freewheels on this linguistic razor's edge.
Air vibrates, ozone crackles.
Border people have the Janus-face,
memories of advance, retreat and slavery.
Anarchy is daily meat,
bodies taut from snapping food, on the run.
Nervous shifting into dying languages,
easing over shibboleths,
slashing, defining.

Where does Scotland begin?
Find Absaroka on a modern map.
Border men and women trudge nationhood
in bundles and rags.
Kurdistan haunts Bonn,
Connemara blood mixed with London cement and mortar.
Armenia weeps over redwood tables in California.

A Zen master could not
tell a dead leaf from a living butterfly.
Geographical leaf, metaphysical butterfly.
Death harries life, mingles and departs.
Frontiers beyond fire and gunshot,
dagger and famine.
Death defines what life blurs,
when we all leap clear of borders,
boundless, free.